Unique Like Me

Written and Illustrated By Sandra Baker

WTL INTERNATIONAL

Unique Like Me

Library and Archives Canada Cataloguing in Publication

Baker, Sandra, 1974-, author
Unique like me / Sandra Baker.

ISBN 978-1-927865-25-5 (paperback)

1. Individual differences--Juvenile literature. 2. Identity (Psychology)--Juvenile literature. 3. Self-perception--Juvenile literature. I. Title.

BF697.B34 2016   j155.2'2   C2016-906448-4

Published by
WTL International
930 North Park Drive
P.O. Box 33049
Brampton, Ontario
L6S 6A7 Canada

www.wtlipublishing.com

ISBN 978-1-927865-25-5

Printed in the USA and Canada

10 9 8 7 6 5 4 3 2 1

This book is dedicated
in loving memory to my parents
Mr. and Mrs. Edward and Joan Hill.
We miss you very much!

xoxo

I do not look like Mommy. Isn't that funny?

I don't look like Daddy or my cousin Maddy.

I do not look like Grandma. It's clear to see.
But guess what? Grandma loves me for me.

6

I do not look like Grandpa, but that is okay.
What matters to me most is that we always play.

My Uncle says it's okay and doesn't find it odd that I don't look like my cousins Nathan or Todd.

8

**My hair is different compared to others.
It doesn't even look anything like my brother's.**

We love it when our auntie reads us this book because it's about our different looks.

I like dogs a lot because they don't stare.
All they do is show that they care.

It's great to have a mother's pride,
And know that she'll be by your side.

We are twins but we have different grins.

My parents chose me and we live in harmony.

I may look different but I think it's neat
That each person has a heartbeat.

15

**This is my family as different as can be.
Yes, I'm unique, but I'm happy just being me!**

16

I stand out. This is very true.
But no matter who you are, you're unique too!

17

My Family Map

Draw an x on the country where you live.

Use different colours for each country that your parents and grandparents are from. Don't forget to colour the country where you live.

Use differnt colours for family born in different countries

Mommy's Family	Daddy's Family
☐ Mommy	☐ Daddy
☐ Grandma	☐ Grandma
☐ Grandpa	☐ Grandpa

CPSIA information can be obtained at www.ICGtesting.com
Printed in the USA
LVIW01n0751070217
523444LV00001B/1